The Search Committee Handbook

The Step-by-Step Guide to Hiring Your Next Minister

Don Viar

Created in the United States of America

Distributed by
Ekklesia Services, LLC
410 South Lowe Avenue
Cookeville, TN 38501

www.MinisterMatch.com

TM – "The Minister Hiring Process," "Minister Match" and "Minister Wanted" are trademarks of Ekklesia Services, LLC.

This book is dedicated to my family,
Ashley, Sarah, Rachel and Savannah.

"Children's children are the crown of old men;
and the glory of children are their fathers"
Proverbs 17:6 KJV

Contents

Preface

This document provides detailed guidance for congregations who are in search of a new minister. It serves as a step-by-step instruction manual to help elders, deacons, search committees and others conduct a thorough and orderly search process. While there can sometimes be a conflict between having a highly structured process and being Spirit-led, my prayer is that God will work within the process to help each congregation find the minister He has called for them.

While there may be many groups who benefit from the study of this content, the primary target audience is a Church of Christ congregation in the United States with 250+ members who seek to fill a full-time ministry position. Other religious groups, nonprofits or smaller congregations may still find value in the content, but may also need to modify the process to fit their needs.

I would recommend that leaders of The Minister Hiring Process ™ read through this handbook once in its entirety to develop an overall understanding of the approach. Then, leaders can work through the handbook a second time on a phase-by-phase basis to guide them through each part of their search.

 Along the way, the handbook references numerous documents and templates from the MinisterMatch.com website. When you see this symbol, go to the site and search for the text shown to the left of this symbol. A complete listing is also provided in Appendix A.

Acknowledgements

I want to thank God for the providential opportunity that led to the creation of Minister Match, the Minister Hiring Process and this handbook. I have no doubt that He had a hand in my being asked to serve on two search committees at the same time.

A book like this would not be possible without the help and support of my family and friends. I am grateful for the patience and support of my wife, Ashley, over these last six months as I put both the book and the company together. I am also grateful for our three daughters, Sarah, Rachel and Savannah, who truly continue to grow in grace and beauty and motivate me to keep pushing harder.

I am grateful for my father, Jim Viar, who served as both an encourager and advisor for this project. As I wrote this book, he also served as the chair of a search committee for his congregation. His practical insights helped ground the book in the reality of the ups and downs of a minister search.

I am profoundly grateful to my friend and fellow search committee member, Phillip Burr. Together we endured the pain that led directly to the creation of Minister Match. He has patiently proofread draft after draft of this material to make sure it rings true for a search committee member.

Last and certainly not least, I am grateful for the ongoing support and friendship of our ministers at Jefferson Avenue Church of Christ – Buddy Johnson and John Nichols. Both have been constant sources of inspiration, instruction and practical guidance from the perspective of a minister.

Introduction

1 Corinthians 14:33 says, "For God is not a God of disorder but of peace." While the original context of that passage clearly has to do with worship, it can be applied in a broader sense to how we conduct the affairs of the church at large. The hiring of a new minister is a unique and potentially stressful time in the life of a congregation. Hiring decisions have an enormous impact on the congregation's long-term health and future. Thoughtful, well-executed searches can bless the congregation for generations to come, while the wrong hire can lead to stagnation, decline and even division.

The Need for a Better Process

A recent poll from Lifeway Research[1] said that the average minister's tenure in a Baptist church is 3.6 years. Anecdotal experience in the Churches of Christ suggests that we are on a similar trajectory. Why is it that some congregations find ministers with tenures that last decades while others find themselves searching for a new minister every few years? The answer (at least in part) might have something to do with HOW the congregation hired their minister.

The process of hiring a minister is different from hiring within a business or an academic environment and brings a unique set of challenges. Just a few of these challenges are:

---

[1] Lifeway Research, Dennis Cook, July 18, 2011
2 As a matter of full disclosure, I also own and operate this site.

- A lack of experience within the congregation on how to hire a minister.
  - How will you pick your search committee?
  - What steps will you go through to find a minister?

- The reality that church members are often not "connected" with the ministerial community at large and know relatively few potential candidates.
  - How will you identify and develop candidates?

- The fatigue that sets in for both the committee and the candidates during the course of the hiring process can lead to a rush to judgment by both parties.
  - How will you evaluate the candidates, and who has the authority to make the final decision?

These sorts of issues have meant that minister searches are often unstructured, poorly executed and confusing processes that result in weak candidate pools and a less than optimal fit between the congregation and the minister. Congregations often wind up with a minister whose doctrine, personality, teaching method or leadership style does not match with their culture.

Both parties go through an uncomfortable "honeymoon" phase where they hope things will get better. Eventually, a segment of the congregation decides that it is time to make a change and they start campaigning for one. A year or two may go by before there is consensus on the need for change. The net results are shorter minister tenures, increased hiring costs, dysfunction within the congregation and maybe even division.

The Search Committee Handbook is designed to lead an eldership or search committee through an orderly, structured process to find their "right" minister and break this cycle. We call this method The Minister Hiring Process ™.

The Minister Hiring Process

The Minister Hiring Process consists of five distinct phases, with each phase running to completion before the next phase can begin. These phases are:

Planning — Clearly defining your needs, budget, search process, etc.

Development — Identifying and attracting qualified candidates.

Selection — An expeditious evaluation of the candidate pool to pick a nominee.

Introduction — The nominee's visit with the congregation and the job offer.

On-Boarding — Helping the minister acclimate to the congregation and community.

We will explore each of these phases in detail in the remaining sections of this book.

Timeline

Everyone wants to know, "How long will this process take?" The search for a new minister may take anywhere from six to eighteen months (or longer). The average search typically takes about nine months to complete. This timeframe assumes that the congregation is stable, that the committee is actively meeting, that the congregation has committed the financial resources to support the search, that candidates are being actively recruited and that the compensation package is competitive.

The time required to complete the Planning Phase and begin the Development Phase can be tightly scheduled at the start of the search. Similarly, the timeline for the Selection through On-Boarding Phases can be closely managed given a relative starting date.

The real mystery of the timeline will be the length of time in the middle that it takes to complete the Development Phase.

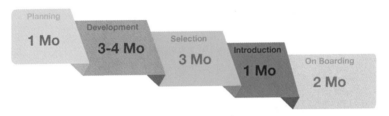

The development of a qualified pool of candidates is without a doubt the most challenging aspect of the minister search process. Specifically, what will constitute a suitable pool of candidates for the committee to consider? How many qualified candidates will you need before you move on to the Selection Phase? How are you going to find these candidates? On your own or with a search firm?

Logically, the deeper and better qualified the pool, the more likely you are to find an outstanding fit for your congregation.

My prayer is that whether you choose to conduct your search alone or in partnership with someone like Minister Match, that the resources and information in this handbook will help you find an outstanding minister for your congregation.

Yours in Christ,

Don Viar
Cookeville, Tennessee

Section I – The Planning Phase

"For which of you, desiring to build a tower, does not first sit down and count the cost, whether he has enough to complete it? Otherwise, when he has laid a foundation and is not able to finish, all who see it begin to mock him, saying, 'This man began to build and was not able to finish.'" – Luke 14:28-30 ESV

Prayer

Pray for God's hand to be upon the process as you search for a new minister. Pray for the elders as they establish a vision for the position and the search process. Pray for wisdom as they select search committee members. Pray for the search committee members as they consider their acceptance of this important responsibility.

Successful searches are carefully planned and executed to attract and retain the best candidates. The Planning Phase begins with a clear vision and leadership from the elders who then form a search committee to carry out the actual search process. Once formed, the search committee will spend time in prayer and getting organized and then wrap up the planning process for the Development Phase. The entire Planning Phase will typically take about a month to complete.

CHAPTER 1

Establish a Vision

It is vital that the elders begin the search process with a clear, unified vision of the qualities and qualifications of the person that they seek to hire. To establish this vision, the elders should meet and address the following six topics:

- ☐ Internal assessment
- ☐ The job description
- ☐ The salary range
- ☐ The search resources
- ☐ The search budget
- ☐ The "charge"

Internal Assessment

Before you start the hiring process, the elders should meet to perform a retrospective and introspective assessment of your ministry needs.

For starters, why are you searching for a new minister? Did the last minister leave after a short tenure? Did they leave under duress? What is the current attitude of the congregation towards your ministers? It may be necessary for the elders to address these issues before beginning the search for a new minister.

Next, the elders should discuss the underlying need for the ministry position. Make sure that there is still general agreement on the need to **hire** someone (on a full-time or part-time basis) to fill this role. Don't get halfway into the search for a new minister only to have one of your elders say, "Why do we even need this person?" or "Couldn't some of our members handle this responsibility?"

The Job Description

Once the need is established, the elders should clearly define the roles, responsibilities and minimum qualifications of the prospective minister. It is important that the elders agree on the "big" items (i.e., the number of sermons to be preached or Bible classes to be taught each month, counseling responsibilities, visitation responsibilities, etc.). There should also be agreement on what you will consider to be the minimum qualifications (e.g., degree level, experience, marital status, etc.).

This should be documented in the form of a written job description that can eventually be shared with your search committee and candidates. Some elderships provide their search committee with a solid "rough draft" of the job description and solicit the committee's input on the final details.

It may also be helpful to search on the Internet for job descriptions written by other congregations. Make sure that the responsibilities placed on your minister will be in line with similar roles in other congregations. Be sure to allow for periodic breaks in teaching and preaching to help your minister stay sharp and fresh.

The Salary Range

It is absolutely critical that the elders establish a clear, budget-conscious, market-competitive salary range at the outset of the search process.

The elders should review published ministry salary surveys from places such as Abilene Christian University's Siburt Institute (http://www.acu.edu/siburt-institute/resources/salarysurvey) when setting a target range. Unless the congregation has been extremely diligent in providing merit increases for its ministerial staff, current salaries in the labor market may surprise you. While you are obviously constrained by your church budget and your stewardship over those funds, you also want to make sure that you are going to be market-competitive in your salary offering.

Some elders might push back on the idea of establishing or sharing a salary range and say, "The salary will be based on experience." That is naive in today's job market and top candidates will certainly enquire about the salary potential before agreeing to be included in the search process. The lack of a pre-determined range often signals indecisiveness, an immature search process, or a below-market salary. If you want top candidates to apply, set a salary range.

The Search Support Resources

There are a number of service firms, tools and databases available to conduct, support or assist the search committee in its efforts.

Search Firms

Congregations with established budgets may want to engage a minister search firm (like Minister Match) to support their search committee. While you may wonder if your congregation can afford a search firm, you will probably be pleasantly surprised. Congregations with at least 250 members can typically use the money originally budgeted for the minister's salary to cover the cost of engaging a search firm and pay for an interim minister.

Working with search firms can offer the following benefits to the search committee:

- **<u>Identification of qualified and motivated candidates</u>**. A search firm often has pre-existing knowledge about potential candidates and can implement an outreach strategy to identify additional candidates outside of a congregation's personal networks. This may include advertising, phone calls, emails and other tactics to uncover new candidates—especially candidates that are not actively job hunting.

- **Third-party objectivity**. A search firm is an objective participant in the process. This can be particularly helpful in cases where the search committee is divided on issues or on a set of final candidates. Third-party objectivity is also useful when conducting reference checks on your finalists.

- **Efficient processes**. Working with a search firm can free up the valuable time of the search committee members. For instance, since Minister Match created The Minister Hiring Process, we are experts at executing the search process and customizing all of the supporting tools and templates to fit a congregation's specific needs.

If there is interest in using a search firm, **I would highly recommend that you engage with one prior to the formation of your search committee**. Minister Match would welcome the opportunity to speak with you about our Guided Search services if you have such an interest. For more information, see our website (http://www.ministermatch.com/guided-search).

Online Resources

One of the reasons I started Minister Match was due to the lack of a single unified resource on the Internet that offered minister search resources for the Churches of Christ. On the Minister Match website (http://www.MinisterMatch.com) we offer the following resources:

- **Job Board** – If you follow the Minister Hiring Process (either on your own or in a Guided Search), you can post your job for free on the Minister Match site (http://www.ministermatch.com/ministers/featured-positions).

- **Minister Database** – Ministers can register to have their resumé included in our database for potential full-time, part-time, interim or guest-speaking opportunities.

- **Document Templates** – Throughout this handbook you will see references to various templates and best practices on the Minister Match website. Use them to jump-start your own efforts and reduce the workload on your search committee.

- **Group Forums** – Discussion boards where elders, deacons and search committees can share insights with their peers in public or private forums.

- **Training and Coaching** – We offer a variety of free training webinars for search committees and elders on the Minister Hiring Process. Congregations that elect to pursue the Minister Hiring Process on their own may want to engage Minister Match for a half-day training seminar for their search committee.

In addition, several church-related universities offer access to a database of their ministry-related alumni. You typically must be a registered member of their site to access the database. Just keep in mind that the people in a school database may or may not be actively in the job market.

The Search Budget

With all factors having been considered, the elders need to establish a budget for the search process itself. Even in simple searches, the committee will incur costs for items such as advertising, candidate and search committee travel costs, food for long committee meetings, etc. The elders need to make sure that the search committee will have all of the resources (financial and non-financial) that they will need to be successful.

Committee Charge

Last, the elders need to decide on the scope of the responsibility they are delegating to the search committee. I call this the "charge." For instance:

- How many candidates should the committee present to the elders or the congregation?
  - A single, well-vetted name or multiple candidates?
- Who will decide on the final candidate?
  - The committee, the elders or the congregation?
  - If it is the committee, should they reach a unanimous decision or a consensus decision?
- Does the committee chair extend the final job offer or will the elders?

In other words, what constitutes "success" for the committee and when will their work be done?

Based upon all of their work in the search process, I typically believe that the committee will be in the best position to evaluate the candidate pool and make an informed decision on behalf of the congregation. **For this reason, I would recommend that the elder's charge ask the committee to identify and nominate a single "consensus" candidate.** Consensus means that there is a general agreement among the committee to call a particular candidate but not necessarily a unanimous decision.

Once the committee has a nominee, the elders might then expect to help shape and deliver the actual job offer.

Regardless, the charge should be written down for the committee so that they can refer back to it for continued confirmation that they are on the right path in the months ahead.

CHAPTER 2

Form a Search Committee

Once the elders have clearly established a vision for the position, they are ready to delegate the logistics of the search process to a committee of capable members. It is hard to overstate the importance of selecting the right people for this task. In forming the search committee the elders need to consider:

- ☐ The size of the committee,
- ☐ The attributes of a successful committee chair and
- ☐ The demographics and personality traits of potential committee members.

Once appointed, the chair will need to implement some organization prior to the initial search committee meeting.

Committee Size

How many people should be on the search committee? The smaller the search committee, the tougher it will be to have representation from all of the major constituencies of the congregation. On the other hand, the larger the search committee, the more difficult it will be to coordinate calendars, reach a consensus for decision-making and maintain the confidentiality of the search process. Depending on the size of the congregation and the nature of the minister being hired, I typically recommend that search committees have between five and nine members, with seven being the ideal in most situations.

Chair Selection

The elders should start by appointing a member of the congregation to chair the search committee. This should be a deliberate decision on the part of the elders and not left to a popularity vote among committee members or an "I'll do it if no one else will" sort of decision.

The chair should be a capable person with gifts for administration, collaborative leadership and organization. They should be highly respected within the congregation and have the trust of the majority of the members. While experience with prior minister searches is not required, ideally they would at least have some experience with hiring or supervision in some other capacity.

Special consideration should be given before asking an elder to serve as chair (or even to be on the search committee), and in most cases I would recommend against it for three reasons:

1. From a time commitment perspective, it is very difficult to both shepherd and serve on a search committee. One of the roles will suffer.
2. An elder serving on the committee wields an enormous amount of influence over the search committee itself. Committee members may feel pressure to acquiesce to the elder's desires or assume that the elder's opinions represent those of the entire eldership.
3. An elder serving on the committee can also create a stressful dynamic within the eldership should there be disagreement about the hiring process, recommended candidates or the compensation package.

As in Acts 6:3, when the apostles appointed deacons, let's find people *"of good repute, full of the Spirit and of wisdom, whom we will appoint to this duty."*

Member Selection

To the extent possible, the committee should represent the diversity of the group to be served by the minister being hired. Demographics such as age, years of church membership, gender, ethnicity and marital status should be considered when selecting members for the search committee. Avoid placing a husband-and-wife team on the committee if at all possible (both to help represent more families and to avoid "bloc" votes).

For instance, if you are hiring a pulpit minister, you would want senior adult, mid-life, young married and young adult members on the committee. You would want a mix of men and women: deacons, teachers, ministry leaders and lay-members. The committee should reflect the entire membership of the congregation.

Likewise, if you are hiring a youth minister, you would want youth fathers and mothers, young men and young women, youth deacons and teachers to be a part of the committee. We tell our youth that they are not just the "church of tomorrow" but also the "church of today" — give them a seat in this very important process!

You may also want to consider the inclusion of one or more members of your existing ministry team (if applicable). As fellow ministers, your staff can provide valuable insights on the search process as well as help you connect with various minister networks. Whether you include them on the committee or not, as future co-workers, it is important that your existing staff feels connected with this process.

In the end, you are looking for people who can set aside their personal agendas and look at candidates in an objective manner. You want people who will speak up in committee meetings without being domineering or argumentative, yet are able to listen thoughtfully to other points of view. You also need people who are willing to make decisions based upon consensus. Consensus means that a committee member might not be very enthusiastic about a particular decision, but he or she would nevertheless be willing to acquiesce to the majority. They would support the committee's decisions and not work to undermine the committee's efforts.

It is also vital to select people who can be trusted to maintain the confidence and confidentiality of the search process in perpetuity. Throughout the course of the search, committee members will receive names and details about candidates that could be damaging should they be ever be disclosed publicly. As an extension of the church in its role as an employer, the committee members must never reveal this information.

Member Commitment

The people who are asked to serve on your search committee must understand that this is a very serious commitment of their time and energy — they will meet often; some of the meetings will last three to four hours (or longer); they will be asked to sacrifice some weekends; and there may be some travel involved. The level of commitment is often great enough that search committee members find it necessary to take a break from other time-consuming church (and non-church) activities and responsibilities.

The elders should work in partnership with the chair to identify potential committee members. Members should not be approached until both the chair and the elders are in agreement on asking a particular member to serve. Ultimately, the chair should make the approach to the member and ask for their involvement. Be sure to clearly outline the time commitment, meeting schedule and other logistics related to serving. Only accept a member who can enthusiastically accept and commit to the process.

Search Committee Organization

To help ensure that the search committee conducts its business as efficiently as possible, the committee should set up some internal organization for communication, meeting preparation and information distribution.

Committee Secretary

Once the members have been selected, someone should be asked to serve as the committee secretary. The secretary should be charged with publishing minutes to each meeting ahead of the next meeting. Those minutes should document committee discussions, decisions and preparations to be made before the next meeting.

Point of Contact (PoC)

If you are working with a search firm, all potential candidates should be directed to apply with your designated point of contact within the firm. Otherwise, select a member of the committee (often the chair) who will serve as the point of contact (PoC) for potential applicants. It is important that you pick someone who will be professional both in verbal and written communications with the candidates. A candidate's first impression of your congregation will often be determined by their interaction with the PoC. Disorganized or unprofessional communications will scare away your top candidates.

All communications and interactions between the committee and the candidate should be funneled through the PoC. If contacted directly by a candidate, committee members should refer them back to the PoC to ensure consistency of communications with each candidate.

Member Information Sheet

To help committee members (and eventually candidates) get to know each other better, ask each committee member to fill out an information sheet ahead of the first committee meeting. In addition to basic contact information, you might include details about their family, hometown, places they have worshiped in the past, etc.

File Sharing

The committee should establish an online resource to share and edit files. Numerous services such as Dropbox, Google Drive, Apple iCloud and Microsoft Sky Drive make this easier and cheaper than ever. Consider setting up permissions that allow the chair, secretary and PoC to store and edit documents before they are ready for distribution to the rest of the committee. (E.g., do not share the candidate application packets with everyone until it is time to do so.) If you are working with a search firm, they might set this up for you free of charge.

Congregation Updates

The chair should make sure that the congregation receives brief status updates throughout the course of the search process. Provide the first update shortly after the committee has been formed and then again at the end of each phase in the hiring process. Let them know that you are making progress but avoid committing to specific details or setting specific timelines. For instance, at the end of the Planning Phase you might say, "*We are preparing to advertise the position and start actively recruiting candidates. We expect it to take several months to assemble our candidate pool.*"

Solicit their prayers for the upcoming phase of the search process and give them something specific to pray for (e.g., "*Pray for God to work providentially through this process and bring us the right minister.*").

Elder Updates

The chair and the elders should discuss how often the elders will be updated on the progress of the search. At a minimum, the chair should probably meet with the elders once each month to provide a brief update similar to the congregation update but with greater specifics. It is important that the committee keep the elders abreast of their progress throughout the search. Building a strong relationship between the elders and the committee will pay big dividends for everyone at the end of the search when the committee is ready to fulfill its charge.

Meeting Preparation

In preparation for each meeting, the chair should take the lead on the preparation of any documents to be discussed or presented.

Meeting Agendas

Ahead of each meeting, the chair or secretary should send out a written agenda via e-mail. The agenda should outline all of the material to be covered and decisions to be made at the meeting. Provide advance copies of any documents to be discussed so that committee members have ample time to review them prior to the meeting.

In preparation for the first meeting, the following checklist might help the chair adequately prepare:

Initial Committee Meeting Preparation Checklist
- ☐ Initial committee meeting agenda
- ☐ Copies of the member information sheets
- ☐ Copies of the charge from the elders
- ☐ The Minister Hiring Process overview (copies made)
- ☐ Preliminary meeting schedule
- ☐ Job description (draft)
- ☐ Job advertisement (draft)

CHAPTER 3

Initial Committee Meeting

As you might imagine, the first meeting of the search committee is extremely important for a variety of reasons. First, it will help the committee members get to know each other better — especially if they come from the diverse demographics recommended in Chapter 2. Second, this meeting will set the tone for the many more to follow. It needs to be highly organized and to help the committee fully understand their assignment. Third, the meeting should clearly communicate the structure and approximate timeline of the search process itself.

Initial Committee Meeting Agenda

A sample initial committee meeting agenda is available on MinisterMatch.com, but here are some of the items that need to be included:

- ❑ Introductions
- ❑ Prayer
- ❑ Committee charge
- ❑ Confidentiality
- ❑ Hiring process review
- ❑ Internal candidates
- ❑ Next steps

Member Introductions

If the members don't know each other already, the chair should take a few minutes at the outset of the meeting and ask the members to introduce themselves and tell the group why they agreed to serve.

If you have engaged with a search firm, representatives should be on hand at this first meeting. Introduce their representatives and provide a background on the search firm. Clearly outline what their role will be in the hiring process.

Prayer

Each meeting should be opened and/or closed with time spent in prayer. At this initial meeting:

- Pray for God to work providentially through the process.
- Pray for the search committee members.
- Pray for the congregation during this time of transition.
- Pray for the candidates, their families and their current congregations.
- Pray for wisdom within the search committee's decisions.

Charge From the Elders

A representative from the elders should join the committee for the first few minutes of the meeting to thank the committee members for their service and to provide the committee with a copy of the written "charge" (see Chapter 1). The elder should read the charge and field questions from the committee to make sure that everyone is on the same page.

Confidentiality

The committee members should be told of the need for absolute confidentiality both during and in perpetuity **AFTER** the search process is over. They have been chosen, at least in part, because of their ability to maintain the confidence and confidentiality of the information entrusted to them. Even something as simple as mentioning that a particular candidate applied for the position years after the fact can be damaging both to the candidate and the minister you eventually hired.

With that in mind, the committee should discuss what information they can share with their spouses. Generally speaking, the fewer people that know the specific details about the candidates, the better. Again, you do not want to do anything that would jeopardize these candidates in their current positions.

Committee members need to be careful to protect access to their computers, tablets and smartphones that may contain information related to the search. If at all possible, the committee should refrain from printing hard copies of candidate information. If copies are printed, offer to shred all documents at the conclusion of the search to ensure maximum privacy for the candidates.

The Minister Hiring Process Overview

Prior to the initial meeting, committee members should have received a copy of the Minister Hiring Process overview or *The Search Committee Handbook* that outlines your overall approach to this search. Discuss the five major phases of the search process and the major tasks and milestones associated with them. Be sure to note where you are currently within the Planning Phase.

Preliminary Meeting Schedule

The chair should also review the preliminary timeline for the remainder of the search process. Ask the committee members to confirm their availability for the key dates outlined. Discuss how certain aspects of the timeline can be relatively firm, while others may require some fluidity.

At a minimum, you should be able to set the dates for your remaining meetings of the Planning Phase. I would also recommend that you go ahead and reserve dates for the initial candidate review meeting and the Round 2 remote interviews of the Selection Phase. While they are subject to change, setting these dates now will help set an expectation for the overall search timeline.

Handling Internal Candidates

The committee needs to be prepared for the possibility that an existing minister, member of the congregation or relative of a member might apply for the position. Decide in this first meeting how these sorts of "internal" situations will be handled. Will these candidates receive preferential treatment, or will they flow through the process like every other candidate?

While every situation is unique, the right course of action probably hinges on the perceived strength of the candidate and the committee's ability to reach a consensus on that point. If the committee feels that the candidate is a very strong candidate, then it might make sense to move that candidate straight into Round 2 of the selection process and have a quick series of interviews and meetings with the candidate. There is no sense in going through a lengthy search if you already have the right candidate in-house. Otherwise, if the committee is uncertain about a candidate's qualifications, it is best to include them in the search process just like any other qualified candidate.

Either way, clearly communicate the committee's plans to any of these candidates that might apply.

Next Steps

Last, as part of this initial committee meeting, you need to briefly discuss the remaining tasks and documents to be created by the committee as part of the Planning Phase. At a minimum, this will include the following:

- The job description,
- The job advertisement,
- The congregation information packet,
- A strategy for the Development Phase, and
- The minimum number of qualified candidates needed for the candidate pool prior to the start of the Selection Phase.

Drafts of the job description and job advertisement should be distributed at this initial meeting so that the committee can review them ahead of the next meeting.

As you can see, this is a lot of information to cover in the first meeting. Plan on it taking about 90 minutes to cover everything. Some committees actually choose to schedule 2-3 hours for their initial meeting so that they can jump right into editing the job description and the job advertisement. If you elect to go that route, be sure to distribute drafts of both documents to the committee ahead of the meeting.

| CHAPTER 4 |

Planning Wrap-up

Typically, the committee will need one or two additional meetings to wrap up the planning process for the Development Phase. Specifically, they need to finalize the following:

❑ The job description
❑ The job advertisement
❑ Congregation information packet
❑ Development planning
❑ Congregational survey (optional)
❑ Candidate questionnaire (optional)

Whenever possible, the committee should try to distribute information via e-mail or through a file-sharing resource to facilitate edits and feedback. This will reduce the time spent as a group trying to wordsmith a document.

I have already discussed the job description, but let's briefly look at the rest of the items mentioned above.

Job Advertisement

The job advertisement will be used for all print and online postings to announce the job opening. The advertisement should provide basic details such as:

- The job title,
- Name and location of the congregation,

- Minimum criteria for application (degree, experience, marital status, etc.),
- What to submit for consideration (resumé, references, sample lessons, etc.),
- How to apply and
- A deadline for application.

Avoid the urge to detail the job description and all of the duties and responsibilities of the position. Focus on why a candidate would want to live in your community and work with your congregation. Sell them on your strengths and then tell them how to apply. If you like, you can always have a copy of the job description available for download from your website for those that are looking for more detail.

Congregation Information Packet

Put yourself in the shoes of a potential applicant for this position. What information would you need to know about your congregation before you applied for the position? You probably would want to know things such as:

- The size of the congregation and trends in membership over the last 5 or 10 years;
- A list of the current staff along with their titles and tenure with the congregation;
- A list of the elders and deacons;
- Something about the demographics of the church members (age, education levels, etc.);
- The congregation's style of worship;
- A list of ministries and programs offered;
- The annual budget; etc.

Now take a look at your church website. How well does it convey these sorts of details to an applicant? If the answer is "not well," the committee may need to create an information packet to share with candidates. This might be something as simple as a Word document or a brochure that could be e-mailed to a candidate.

Development Planning

At your initial committee meeting, the chair should have asked the committee to start thinking about the Development Phase. There are really two main issues that the committee needs to decide at this stage of the process:

1. How is the committee going to identify and qualify potential candidates?
2. Are there a minimum number of qualified candidates that the committee wants to have in the pool before they start the Selection Phase?

How Will You Identify and Qualify Potential Candidates?

Minister searches typically employ some combination of advertising, networking and recruiting to develop a suitable pool of candidates. While advertising is important to the process, very rarely will your ideal candidate respond to an ad. Read through Chapter 5 and develop a strategy for how the committee will find candidates.

What exactly constitutes a "qualified candidate"? At a fundamental level, a qualified candidate is someone who meets the minimum qualifications outlined in the job description. Often, however, a committee will have a number of additional criteria that will shape their perception of a "qualified" candidate. Do you want someone with conservative or progressive theology? Or, do you want someone with experience in similar-sized churches? Whatever these additional criteria may be, the committee should discuss what a qualified candidate will look like ahead of time. Ask the secretary to document it for future reference by the committee members.

How Many Candidates Do You Need?

How many qualified candidates should you have in the candidate pool before you start the Selection Phase? This really is a question for the committee to decide. Some positions literally attract hundreds of qualified applicants, while others struggle to find more than a handful. Obviously, the more restrictive you are in your qualifications, the harder it will be to find candidates.

For mainstream congregations in the southern U.S. seeking to fill major ministry positions without overly restrictive qualifications, here are some suggested minimum candidate goals:

Members	Qualified Candidates
< 100	25
101-300	40
300-500	50
500-1,000	75
1,000+	100+

The committee may start the Development Phase with the expectation that it will take three months to build a quality candidate pool. However, if you find that your initial applicants are too few or are under-qualified for the position, then the committee may need to extend the application deadline, adjust the wording and placement of the job advertisement, adjust the salary range or engage with a search firm to develop additional candidates.

Congregational Survey (optional)

The committee may wish to survey the congregation for their input at the outset of the search process. Surveys can both help the committee better understand the congregation's desires and help the congregation feel like they have a connection to the search process. Focus the survey on the skills and experience levels that they would most desire in your next minister.

To increase your participation rates, consider using multiple types of media to distribute the survey. Have hard copies printed up and ready for pickup in your church foyers or for handout in Bible classes. Also consider using an online survey site such as Survey Monkey (www.surveymonkey.com) to reach members who are connected to the Internet.

Surveys can be distributed during the Planning Phase and the results compiled prior to the start of the Selection Phase. The survey should not hold up the start of your Development Phase.

Candidate Questionnaire (optional)

The committee may also wish to create a questionnaire for candidates to complete as part of the application process. Candidate questionnaires are common in minister searches and are a great way to go beyond the standard resumé without committing to a formal interview.

Typically, the questions will revolve around a few common themes:

- The candidate's views on a few of the current issues within the church and society at large (e.g., women's roles in the church, instrumental music, homosexuality, etc.)
- The candidate's personal faith (what they study, family devotionals, prayer life, etc.)

- The candidate's personal life (hobbies, divorces, bankruptcies, criminal record, etc.)
- The candidate's network of peers in the church at large (e.g., where they have spoken or who they have invited to speak, etc.)

I would recommend limiting your questionnaire to no more than 15 questions. Focus on items that you expect would be the most revealing for your congregation. Encourage candidates to go beyond simple answers and to provide you with some narrative when it is appropriate.

Section II – The Development Phase

"While walking by the Sea of Galilee, he saw two brothers, Simon (who is called Peter) and Andrew his brother, casting a net into the sea, for they were fishermen. And he said to them, "Follow me and I will make you fishers of men." Immediately they left their nets and followed him. And going on from there he saw two other brothers, James the son of Zebedee and John his brother, in the boat with Zebedee their father, mending their nets and he called them. Immediately they left the boat and their father and followed him." – Matthew 4:18-19 ESV

Prayer

Pray for God to help you find qualified candidates. Pray for courage as you reach out to people. Pray for encouragement as you encounter rejection during the recruiting process. Pray for patience as you wait for the process to work.

Having laid the proper foundation, it is now time to start the process of finding potential candidates. As mentioned in the last chapter, this will require a combination of advertising, networking and outright recruiting.

CHAPTER 5

Creating a Candidate Pool

Advertising

The very first place you will want to advertise is within your local congregation. Put a copy of the advertisement in your weekly bulletin and on the church website. Ask members of the congregation to share the posting with friends and family that they may have in other congregations. When a potential candidate visits your church website, they should immediately see the job posting and be able to start the application process.

As of 2015, there are also dozens of websites and publications that publish job postings for Church of Christ ministerial positions. Some of these sites are free, while others require a posting fee. Decide where you will advertise and who on the committee will be responsible for posting the ad. If you are working with a search firm, they will typically handle this for you as part of their service.

As of the end of 2014, here are some of the more popular places to advertise your job posting:

Websites

- Minister Match[2]
  - o http://www.MinisterMatch.com
- Minister Wanted[2]
  - o http://www.MinisterWanted.com

---

2 As a matter of full disclosure, I also own and operate this site.

- Harding School of Theology
  - http://hst.edu/our-community/ministry-job-opportunities/
- Lipscomb University
  - http://www.lipscomb.edu/www/search/career
- Abilene Christian University
  - https://cbs-acu-csm.symplicity.com/employers/index.php?s=home&mode=list
- Ohio Valley University
  - http://web.ovu.edu/bible/chlookpg.htm
- Sunset International Bible Institute
  - http://www.sibi.cc/ministers_needed
- Oklahoma Christian University
  - http://www.oc.edu/church-relations/jobs/search-ministry-positions.html
- Lubbock Christian University
  - http://www.lcu.edu/majors-programs/bachelors-degree/bible/ministry-positions.html
- Pepperdine University
  - http://www.pepperdine.edu/churchrelations/resources/jobs/openings.htm
- Heritage Christian University
  - http://www.hcu.edu/resources/churchlisting
- Qohelet Web Ministry
  - http://epreacher.org/jobs.html
- The Small Church Project
  - http://www.thesmallchurchproject.com/small-church-openings/

Publications

- The Christian Chronicle
- The Gospel Advocate
- Truth Magazine

Networking

Networking is the process of utilizing existing contacts and relationships to help the committee uncover potential candidates. Ask members of the congregation, existing ministers, elders and others to provide you with the names of people that you might be able to network with to find candidates. In many cases, these are people who not only know you personally but they also know a little bit about your congregation (your demographics, doctrinal beliefs, leadership, etc.).

- Think about teachers, professors and deans at colleges, universities and schools.
- Think about people who organize conferences and lectureships.
- Think about people who have spoken at your congregation in the past.
- Think about past speakers from prior youth retreats or rallies.
- Think about ministers or elders at places you have worshipped in the past.

Build a list of all possible networking resources as a committee and then assign contacts to specific committee members. The committee should reach out to this network even if you are working with a search firm. Some of your best candidates will often come from the people that you already know.

When you call someone to talk about the position, be prepared to e-mail a copy of the job advertisement and job description to them. Stress that you are only looking for the names of people who have the qualities and attributes of the person you seek and that you would appreciate any names that may come to mind.

Potential candidates should follow the process outlined in the job advertisement to apply for the position.

Recruiting

In most cases, your best candidates are not actively looking for a job, but they may be open to learning more about your position. What happens during the recruiting process will largely depend on if you are working with a search firm or if you have elected to handle the recruitment task internally.

Working with a Search Firm

Recruiting is where a search firm can be worth its weight in gold. Search firms have pre-existing knowledge of potential candidates, databases of potential contacts and the resources to work those prospects. They can help you uncover candidates that your committee might have never found.

With a recruiter, the committee's responsibility during this phase is to be patient. Building a great candidate pool takes time and the search firm needs to be given the time to do its work. Ask for periodic updates, but don't expect to hear much from them on a week-to-week basis unless there is a problem with the quantity or quality of candidates they are finding.

Not Working with a Search Firm

If you are handling the recruitment task internally, then it's time for the committee to dig in and get to work — hard work. The committee needs to compile a list of every congregation in a surrounding 3-4 state region who might have a minister that would be interested in your position. Sites like www.church-of-Christ.org and www.churches-of-Christ.net provide state-by-state listings of congregations. Use these lists as a starting point for your prospect list.

It can be helpful to provide the committee members with a "script" or set of talking points to use when making these calls. You definitely do not want to sound like a telemarketer reading a script, but there should be a structured flow to the call. With a little bit of practice, committee members can be making these calls in no time.

When you first make contact with a potential candidate, it is important to realize that **this is not an interview**. You want qualified candidates to consent to being part of the search. With that in mind, the committee should develop a few talking points about the position, the congregation and the community. Highlight items that will be attractive to potential candidates and encourage them to consider applying. Even if they are not interested, ask if they know someone who might be a good fit for the position.

Plan on making <u>lots</u> of phone calls. The vast majority of the people you call will tell you "no," but a few will express an interest or give you a lead. It is not unusual to make ten phone calls to identify one potential candidate. Your search may require dozens, if not hundreds, of phone calls to build the pool of applicants you seek. The key is to not become discouraged and give up after a couple of dozen calls.

If the committee handles their own recruiting, they should meet periodically throughout the Development Phase to review their results and plan further calls. If the committee is struggling, consider the need to request the help of congregation members who might be in sales or some other profession that has a talent for "working the phones."

It can even be helpful and encouraging for the committee to come together at the church building for a "phone-a-thon" event. Everyone would still make their own individual calls, but from the same room. This way they can listen to each other, learn from each other and celebrate the success of finding a potential candidate. Keep in mind that most of these calls will be to church offices, so that means that at least some of these sessions will need to be during normal business hours.

CHAPTER 6

Initial Candidate Contact

Once a potential candidate has been identified, the committee's point of contact (PoC) will work with them to collect their applications and answer any up-front questions about the search process itself.

Initial Candidate Letter

The PoC should send each candidate an initial introduction letter or e-mail that reiterates:

- How to apply for the position (i.e., what to submit).
- The deadline for application submission.
- The high-level process and timeline of the search process.
- When they might hear next from the committee.
- How to follow up if they have any questions.

If the committee has elected to use a candidate questionnaire, the letter can also be the perfect way to convey it to the candidate and set a deadline for its return.

As candidate documents are received, the PoC should compile them into digital application packets. An application packet would consist of the candidate's resumé, cover letter, references, sample lessons, candidate questionnaire and any other materials that the candidates were asked to provide.

As these application packets are received, the PoC should also send an acknowledgement to the candidate and set the expectations for additional follow-up. Clearly communicate that candidates will not be reviewed or interviewed by the committee until after the application deadline has passed.

Candidate Management

After the initial recruiting contact, <u>no one other than the PoC should engage with potential candidates at this time.</u>

Candidates will sometimes attempt to go directly to an elder, existing minister or the chair to campaign for the position. While well intentioned, it can bias the selection process and should be strongly discouraged. The elders and church staff should have the contact information for the PoC and refer all candidates and questions to that person.

Candidate Pre-Review

If you expect to have a large number of applicants (greater than 50), the recruiter, the chair or the PoC should be tasked with performing a "pre-review" as applications come in. The pre-reviewer should simply classify candidates into a "qualified" or "not qualified" bucket. If the candidate meets the raw qualifications (degree, experience, etc.), then they go into the "qualified" bucket. Candidates in the "not qualified" bucket can be considered by the committee (and should be furnished to them), but in the eyes of the pre-reviewer they do not appear to meet some of the fundamental job qualifications established during the Planning Phase. This will help to lighten the load for the rest of the committee.

Candidate Pooling

It cannot be said strongly enough at this point that the committee as a whole should <u>fight all urges to begin</u>

evaluating candidates as they come in! Do not provide committee members with a list of names or access to the application packets as they trickle in. Do not start researching candidates or discussing their names with anyone. Be patient and let the candidate pool form.

The strength of the Selection Phase is based upon being able to evaluate your candidate pool en masse. Congregations often lose great candidates because they mismanage them. Often a church will engage with a candidate when they apply. They basically interview them and then put them "on hold" for several months while they complete their search process. It implies to the candidate, "You may or may not be who we want, so we will keep looking to see if anyone better comes along." It is far better to wait and engage with candidates when you are actually ready to proceed with the Selection Phase in rapid succession.

Initial Candidate Review

About three weeks prior to your application deadline, the chair or secretary should provide committee members with electronic access to the candidate application packets. Ideally this will be handled through a service such as Dropbox, Google Drive or a dedicated search firm's website so that packets can be updated as additional information is received from the candidates leading up to the deadline.

Committee members should be reminded of the need for confidentiality and encouraged to initially evaluate candidates solely on the basis of what has been submitted. There is no need to "cyber-stalk" a candidate or micro-analyze them at this time. To help committee members document their thoughts and notes on each candidate, provide them with a structured candidate review form.

As they start their initial evaluation, committee members need to consider if the depth and quality of the candidate pool is sufficient enough to warrant moving forward to the Selection Phase. If it is not, then the application date should be extended and plans made to expand the scope of the search process. If it is extended, the PoC should reach out to all applied and potential candidates to let them know about the deadline extension.

This is also the perfect time to provide the committee with a summary of the responses from the congregational survey. As they read through the application packets, it will be helpful for them to be mindful of the qualities and characteristics important to the congregation.

Section III – Selection Phase

"In these days he went out to the mountain to pray and all night he continued in prayer to God. And when day came, he called his disciples and chose from them twelve, whom he named apostles." – Luke 6:12-13 ESV

Prayer

Just as Christ spent time in prayer before selecting His apostles, it would be wholly appropriate for the committee and the congregation to spend time both individually and collectively in prayer at the start of the Selection Phase. Pray for wisdom in your evaluations. Pray for brotherly love and kindness in the committee's deliberations. Ask God to work providentially through the process to help you find the right minister.

The goal of the Selection Phase is to go from a large pool of applicants down to a single nominee over the course of an eight- to twelve-week period of time. The Selection Phase itself is broken down into a series of "rounds" defined as:

- Round 1 – Initial Selection
- Round 2 – Remote Interview

- Round 3 – In-Depth Review
- Round 4 – In-Person Interview
- Round 5 – Nomination

As you can see in the following diagram, there is a "funneling" process as you refine the candidate pool at the end of each round.

		Candidates	Duration
Initial Selection	Round 1	50-100+	1 Day
Remote Interview	Round 2	10-15	2-3 Days
In-Depth Review	Round 3	5-7	3-4 Weeks
In-Person Interview	Round 4	4-5	2-3 Weeks
Nomination	Round 5	1	1 Day

The process depends on having a large and well-qualified candidate pool that allows you to weigh the candidates in light of their peers and draw meaningful comparisons. By design, the process encourages multiple calls, meetings and communications between the candidate and the committee to help both parties get to know each other on a deeper level.

CHAPTER 7

Round 1 – Initial Selection

The initial selection meeting should be set for a date immediately following the application deadline. By now the committee members should have had two to three weeks to study and review the candidate application packets. Committee members should understand that applications will continue to arrive right up until the time of the meeting and that this is perfectly normal and acceptable. Encourage them to come to the meeting prepared to discuss the high-level merits of each candidate.

Initial Selection Meeting Agenda

Committee members should be prepared for an extended meeting that may last three or four hours depending upon the number of applicants. There are three goals for this initial selection meeting:

- ☐ Committee agreement that the candidate pool is ready for the Selection Phase.
- ☐ Identify the top tier of candidates for Round 2 interviews.
- ☐ Develop a standard list of questions to ask each candidate in Round 2.

Agreement on Candidate Pool Depth and Quality
Under no circumstances should you continue the Selection Phase if the committee has any lingering doubts about the depth or quality of the candidate pool. To do so is to risk the quality and integrity of the entire search process. You risk

losing the candidates you have in the pool so far and the time invested to get to this point. It is far better to extend the Development Phase by a month or two than it is to continue the Selection Phase prematurely.

Identify Top Candidates for Round 2
If you have a large number of candidates (50 or more), it may be helpful to take an immediate vote (prior to discussion) on each candidate at the start of the meeting. This will help you see whom the committee has some level of interest in pursuing. Just a simple show of hands by committee members saying yes or no on each candidate will suffice (or if you prefer, use a secret ballot). If someone helped divide the candidates into "qualified" or "not qualified" ahead of time, you may just do a vote on the "qualified" pool and then ask committee members if they have anyone from the "not qualified" pool that requires discussion. The goal here is to see if you can quickly identify the top tiers of the candidate pool.

If you have a smaller pool (or once you have culled the pool as described above), the committee should briefly review and discuss each of the remaining candidates. Various committee members will see different strengths and weaknesses in each candidate. Someone on the committee might personally know a candidate or have some additional insight. Often you will see a clear separation of the candidates into an A-B-C-D stratification.

- A Candidates – The vast majority of the committee approves of moving the candidate forward. You might spend a few minutes discussing an A candidate but save most of your time to discuss other candidates.
- B Candidates – Most committee members approve of moving the candidate forward, but not quite as many as the A candidates. There might be room for discussion about why some committee members voted yes or no

on this candidate, but again, save your time for other candidates.

- C Candidates – The committee seems divided about moving the candidate forward. Depending on the size of your A and B candidate lists and if you still need more Round 2 candidates, you might want to take a second vote on just your C candidates to see if any further stratification occurs. If some rise to the top, focus your discussions around those higher C candidates. Reference the results of your congregational survey to see if any of them have particular traits that were important to the members.
- D Candidates – Most committee members do not approve of moving the candidate forward. That being the case, the committee probably should not waste any time discussing these candidates further.

The goal of Round 1 is to emerge with the top 10-15 candidates or the top 50 percent (depending on the size of your candidate pool) for the Round 2 interviews. If some committee members have doubts about a candidate at this stage, err on the side of including them in the Round 2 discussions.

Round 2 Interview Questions

Before the close of the initial selection meeting, the committee should settle on a list of 10–15 questions to be asked of each candidate in Round 2. Prior to this meeting, the chair should have provided the committee with a list of potential Round 2 questions. The committee needs to edit or approve those questions as they see fit.

It is important to know what you cannot ask as part of the interview process. While churches can address topics that would be taboo or even illegal in a commercial business setting, there are still some areas to avoid. These would include questions about age, physical characteristics, disabilities, chronic illnesses and national origin.

Candidate Rejections

If you think about it, you may connect with dozens (if not hundreds) of ministers throughout the course of this search. In the end, you will have said no to all but one of them! The committee owes each candidate the courtesy of timely updates as the search progresses. How you communicate with them will leave a lasting impression upon them.

Candidates who have not progressed to Round 2 should receive a letter from the recruiter or chair thanking them for their interest in the position, but letting them know that the committee is moving forward in a different direction at this time.

CHAPTER 8

Round 2 – Remote Interviews

The goal of Round 2 is to complete an apples-to-apples evaluation of each candidate so that meaningful comparisons can be brought to light. Time is the enemy in this round. You want to conduct all of the Round 2 interviews in as tight a timeframe as possible. By following a highly structured and tight timetable, subtle (and not-so-subtle) nuances will emerge between the candidates as you see how they respond to the same question or how they budget their time for each answer.

Time Tables

Once the committee has decided on the Round 2 candidates, the Recruiter or PoC should contact each candidate to coordinate a time slot for their 60-minute <u>remote</u> interview. The goal of Round 2 is to conduct a brief interview with every candidate in a 2-3 day period of time if at all possible. While understanding that most committee members will have jobs or other responsibilities, set a date far enough in advance that the committee can clear their calendars and dedicate an entire weekend to the Round 2 interview process (i.e., Friday afternoon, all day Saturday, and Sunday afternoon).

Remote Technology

With today's modern technology, it has never been easier to meet with candidates using video or audio conference bridge services. Services such as Skype, FaceTime, GoToMeeting, WebEx, etc.

make it easy to have a personal video interaction between the committee and the candidates. If video calls are not feasible for the committee or a candidate, consider using a conference phone or conference bridge service like FreeConferenceCall.com to connect.

Also, unless all of your Round 2 candidates are in close proximity to your congregation, be careful about doing some interviews in person and doing others remotely. You can inadvertently introduce bias into the process by treating local candidates differently. It is better to treat everyone the same and use the conference technology even for local candidates.

Round 2 – Invitations

Once the candidate has agreed on a time slot, the recruiter or chair should follow up with a confirmation e-mail along with any instructions for how to connect to the video or audio interview session. The organizer should also offer to conduct a brief trial of the technology ahead of time to make sure that the candidate will be comfortable with the technology on the day of the interview.

Committee Biography

It would also be nice if the organizer could provide the candidates with a brief biography on each committee member ahead of their interview. The biography could be based on the member information forms completed at the start of the search and should tell a little about the committee members and why they were asked to serve on the committee.

Interview Process

Every effort should be made to treat each candidate exactly the same at this stage of the process. Every candidate is interviewed in the same manner. Every candidate has the same length of time. Every candidate is asked the same set of questions in the same order. Every candidate has the same length of time to ask questions at the end of the interview.

Using the predefined Round 2 interview questions created in the last committee meeting, assign specific committee members to ask specific questions.

The chair should start the interview by greeting the candidate and allowing each committee member to briefly introduce themselves. Consider having nametags or place cards in front of the committee members so that the candidates know whom they are speaking with.

After the introductions, the chair should reiterate the schedule for this interview.

> *"The committee members will take turns asking a series of ___ questions for the first 45 minutes. Based upon the number of questions, that will give you (the candidate) approximately ___ minutes to answer each question. If we start to run long on some of the committee's questions, we will skip a few at the end to keep us on time. Regardless, we will save the last 15 minutes of the interview for any questions that you might have for the committee. I will give everyone a warning when we have 30 minutes left in the session."*

The committee members should then proceed to ask their questions in the same order with each candidate.

When it is time for the candidate to ask their questions, the chair should formally give them the floor and remind them of the 15-minute time limit. When there are five minutes remaining in the session, another reminder may be helpful.

At the conclusion of each interview, the chair should thank the candidate for their time and continued interest in the position. If possible, the chair should also indicate when the candidate might expect to next hear something from the committee.

Try to schedule the interviews back-to-back with a 15-minute break for the committee between each candidate. You can probably do three or four interviews in a sitting before pausing for a longer meal break.

Round 2 – Review Meeting Agenda

As soon as possible after the last Round 2 interview (ideally, immediately following its conclusion), the committee should decide which candidates will move forward into Round 3.

Similar to Round 1, before discussion, I recommend that the committee take an immediate vote (by show of hands or secret ballot) on each candidate. This will give you a sense of which candidates have the highest levels of natural interest among the committee. Similar to Round 1, you will hopefully see a clear separation of the candidates into an A-B-C-D sort of classification.

- A Candidates – Again, the vast majority of the committee is in agreement about moving them forward so don't spend much time talking about these candidates.
- B Candidates – While most feel good about these candidates, a few have questions or concerns. Talk briefly about what committee members like or might be concerned about with each candidate. B candidates should be moved forward into Round 3.
- C Candidates – The committee seems evenly split on moving the candidate forward. Like the end of Round 1, if you still need more Round 3 candidates, you might want to take a second vote on just your C candidates to see if any further stratification occurs. Focus your committee discussion around those higher C candidates. Could any of them be "low B" candidates?

- <u>D Candidates</u> – Most committee members do not approve of moving the candidate forward, so don't waste any time discussing these candidates further.

You are not trying to pick "the one" at this stage of the process. There is still a lot of evaluation work to be done in Rounds 3 and 4. At the conclusion of Round 2, you hope to have 5-7 qualified candidates to carry into Round 3.

Candidate Rejections

Candidates who have not progressed to Round 3 should receive a letter from the recruiter or chair thanking them for their interest in the position, but letting them know that committee is moving forward in a different direction at this time.

CHAPTER 9

Round 3 - In-Depth Review

Round 3 is an in-depth review of each candidate to both assess their "fit" for your congregation and to protect the congregation through a "due diligence" process. Candidates will be asked to provide samples of their work for review by the committee and to provide information for background and reference checks. Prior to discussing the actual logistics of Round 3, let's review each of the tasks to be accomplished.

Work Review

Before you hire a minister, the committee needs to be absolutely comfortable with the candidate's doctrinal beliefs and work style. Don't wait until the Sunday morning "try-out worship service" to see if you like their sermon. In fact, in the Minister Hiring Process, you will have decided to hire the candidate **before** you bring them in to meet the congregation.

If you are hiring a pulpit minister, spend time listening to sample sermons and reading their devotionals, bulletin articles and Bible class lessons. If you are hiring a family, youth or children's minister, ask for items such as samples of their lessons, newsletters, annual events calendar, retreat agendas and pre-event communications. If you are hiring a worship leader, ask for copies of past orders of worship, recordings of worship services, etc. Hopefully you get the idea. Even someone right out of college will have something from a class or internship to share with you.

With today's modern technology, the committee should be able to accomplish almost all of this review process remotely. Ask them to provide you with CDs, DVDs, MP3s or links to podcasts, blogs, YouTube videos or other online resources. If necessary, ask them to print and mail a sample of their work. A candidate's inability to provide you with samples of their work should be a red flag.

Don't rely solely on content provided by the candidate. Search the website of their current congregation, YouTube and search engines like Google for additional content. You will hopefully find a mix of current and older content that will provide you with valuable insights about the candidate. Where have they spoken in the past? How do these other lessons compare with what they have already provided you? If possible, start listening to their weekly lessons until you have either eliminated the candidate or have arrived at a nominee.

In rare cases, the committee may have to visit the candidate's current congregation to accomplish this review. While this was once common, it is becoming less and less necessary today. I would encourage both the candidate and committee to avoid a "visit" if at all possible. It slows down the hiring process and can create issues for the candidate in their current congregation. Also, if you visit one candidate, you need to visit all of them out of fairness to the other candidates. If a visit is to be made, wait and do it after the Round 4 in-person interviews.

Committee members should take notes on their reviews that will help them recall specific details when the committee meets to discuss the results.

Background Checks

In many cases, you may not know much about a candidate's history beyond what is on their resumé. In that case, consider the need to perform a full academic, criminal and financial background check on each of the remaining candidates. While some people might be uncomfortable with this sort of "prying" into the life of a fellow church member, it is just part of the due diligence process that a committee needs to follow to protect the congregation.

The facts are that:

- Every six minutes, a convicted criminal tries to attain a position at a nonprofit organization.
- Every 43 hours, at least one convicted sex offender tries to attain a position at a youth-oriented nonprofit organization. *(ChoicePoint senior vice president of screening Bill Whitford)*

❑ Call the candidate's school or university and make sure that they earned the degree that they claim to have.
❑ Run a credit check to make sure they are not in the midst of a potentially embarrassing financial situation.
❑ Do a criminal background check to confirm that they have been forthright about their legal history.

These services are readily available from places such as Secure Search (https://www.securesearchpro.com/index.php/faith-based-organization) and are well worth the cost for the added peace of mind they provide. Be sure to ask the candidate to sign a background search permission form from the vendor before you start any specific inquiries.

Reference Checks

Sometimes congregations will try to skip the referencing part of the process and assume that they already know their candidates well enough. **<u>Don't do it!</u>** This is a vital part of the due diligence process and will help the committee minimize the chance for a surprise after the fact.

The candidates may need to reconfirm their list of references and/or provide additional references as needed. Ask them to provide you with at least one past or present reference in each of the following categories: co-workers, employers, members in congregations where they have served, and long-term character references.

If any of the references are elders or members of the candidate's current congregation, consider asking the recruiter or chair to conduct those reference checks to ensure that full discretion is maintained.

When calling to conduct a reference check, the committee member should identify themselves as a member of your congregation and state the purpose of the call. Ask the reference if this is a convenient time to discuss the candidate or if they would prefer to schedule a time for a later conversation. The call itself will probably take 20-30 minutes to complete.

The committee should use a structured set of questions when calling each reference and encourage the team to document specific answers, quotes and comments from the reference call. When speaking with a reference provided by the candidate, ask them for the names of other people that the committee should consider contacting. These are called "Level 2" references and may be helpful in Round 4 if the committee is having trouble reaching a decision.

Now that we have reviewed the Round 3 tasks, let's move on to the logistics about how to make it all happen.

Round 3 – Candidate Call

At the start of Round 3, the committee's PoC needs to reach out to each of the remaining candidates to provide them with an update and to request some additional information. First, the candidates deserve to know that out of the initial pool of X applicants that they are now one of Y finalists. It tells them that the committee is in the final stages of its process and that you are serious about their candidacy.

Second, the PoC needs to let each candidate know that the committee will make a final hiring decision <u>before</u> they announce a name to the congregation. That means that the committee needs some help and additional information now so that they can fully vet the candidate and be comfortable with both their doctrine and style. In light of what the candidate may have already provided as part of their application packet, this call should cover the following:

1. Their portfolio of online, digital or recorded work samples. If the portfolio is lean, ask the candidate to help you come up with additional ways to sample their work. Decide together if a search committee visit would be needed and/or how to avoid one.

2. Let them know that the committee would like to perform a full academic, criminal and financial background check at this time and that you will send over a form to request their permission.

3. Ask them to review their references in light of the committee's requested references and see if they need to provide any additional names. Stress the committee's appreciation of the need for discretion and that references will only be checked after the sample work reviews and background checks are completed. You will not call references until you are preparing for the final round of interviews.

After the call, send the candidate an e-mail with any requested forms that they need to fill out.

Round 3 Meetings

As you move through the Round 3 process, the committee may find it necessary to meet several times. A suggested structure for these meetings would be:

Meeting 1 – Assign Responsibilities

Form subcommittees of 2-3 members that will work together through the work review and referencing process. Ask subcommittees to focus on specific candidates but stress that all committee members are free to review any candidate. If you have a committee member who is struggling with a particular candidate, it can often be helpful to ask them to serve on the subcommittee for that candidate.

Ask each subcommittee to initially focus on the work review process. They should review all available material and be ready to report back to the whole committee in about a week.

Also, as part of this meeting, assign a committee member (or your recruiter) to head up the task of coordinating background checks for all of the remaining candidates. A single committee member can engage with the background investigation vendor and relay any potentially concerning information to the whole committee as may be needed. This will help ensure maximum privacy for the candidates.

Meeting 2 – Work Review Results/Background Check Results

In the second meeting you will receive the results of the work review from each subcommittee. Specifically,

- What did they review?
- Are they comfortable with the volume of work available for review?
- Are there any doctrinal concerns?

- Were they engaged by the delivery of the material?
- How do they feel about the candidate's style and will it mesh with your congregation?
- Will the committee need to visit the candidate's congregation?

Also, if the background checks are concluded, now is the time to address any potential issues that may have come to light on any of the candidates. If there is nothing to report, that is even better.

Ask the subcommittees to continue forward with the referencing process and give them another week or two to complete that process. If a candidate has already been eliminated or withdrawn from consideration for some reason, reassign the members of that subcommittee to help focus on the remaining candidates.

Meeting 3 – Referencing Results/Final Review
In the third meeting you will receive the results of the reference checks from each subcommittee. Ask the subcommittees to try to provide specific quotes from the references when possible.

As the committee weighs all of the available information, they need to identify their top 4-5 candidates to carry into Round 4. If the committee is on the fence about a candidate, err on the side of bringing them into Round 4. While it may be tempting to have a "favorite" at this stage, continue to fight against a rush to judgment. It is very common for candidates to rise or fall during the Round 4 visit.

Candidate Rejections

Candidates who have not progressed to Round 4 should receive a letter or call from the recruiter or chair thanking them for their interest in the position, but letting them know that committee is moving forward in a different direction at this time.

| CHAPTER 10 |

Round 4 – In-Person Interviews

Round 4 – Invitations

Once the Round 4 candidates have been identified, the recruiter or chair should coordinate an in-person visit for each candidate to come to your facility. This is not a "public" visit for all of the congregation to participate in, but rather a private meeting designed to let the committee and candidate get to know each other better.

While the focus will be on the candidate, consider including the candidate's spouse as part of this visit. This is a perfect opportunity to meet them and to allow them to get a first impression of your congregation and community.

If the visit will require travel on the part of the candidate, the committee should coordinate the details to pay for the trip and any incidental costs. Even if it is just mileage, the congregation should reimburse the candidate for their mileage costs as an initial good-faith investment in the relationship.

In-Person Interview

Schedule 1-2 hours with the candidate to delve into deeper matters about doctrine, the day-to-day responsibilities of the position and additional personal details. If the candidate brought their spouse, invite them to meet with the committee for a few minutes and then have a small group of members (e.g., the spouses of your committee members) take them for a cup of coffee.

As in the Round 2 interview, the committee should develop a set of questions ahead of time that will be asked of each candidate. Some ideas for these questions would be:

- Scenario-based questions that put the candidate into a particular situation that they might encounter in their job. Ask them to walk you through what they think about the situation and how they would handle it.
- Doctrinal questions that explore the candidate's beliefs about a particular issue (e.g., what does it mean for an elder or a deacon to be the husband of one wife? Is baptism really necessary for salvation? etc.).
- Ask them to tell you a little bit about each member of their family. How do they speak of their spouse or children? How would they describe their spiritual life?

This is also an opportune time for the committee members to address any open questions they might have about something in the candidate's application packet or about something they learned in the in-depth review process. If there are any lingering questions about their experience, doctrinal positions or capabilities, now is the time to ask.

Prayer

Either at the beginning or end of the interview, spend time in prayer with the candidate. Pray for the candidate and their family. Pray for their current congregation. Pray for their ministry and for the ministry position to be filled at your congregation. Pray that in all things, God's will be done and that He will make His will known.

Be sure to leave time in the schedule for the candidate to ask any further questions that they might have had since the last interview.

Staff Meeting and Facility Tour

While they are in town, make sure that the candidate has an opportunity to visit with your existing ministers (if applicable). Set up a lunch, dinner or other meeting time for the candidate so that they can talk privately about the congregation, the eldership, the community and anything else that they might want to discuss.

Be sure that they also get a tour of the church building while they are in town. Show them their potential office space, the office and classroom technology, the church library and any other resources that would help them in their day-to-day responsibilities.

Community Tour

Schedule time for some of the committee members to drive the candidate around your community. Show them the schools, parks and natural attractions. Show them neighborhoods where your members live. Show them the restaurants and shopping centers. Show them the businesses and industries where your members work. Bottom line, help them understand the great things about your community and why they would want to consider living there.

Packet of Information

Gather a packet of information about your congregation and your community that the candidate can take home and share with their family. Include information about the congregation such as your written history, the current budget and a membership directory.

Visit your local chamber of commerce or visitors' center to obtain community maps, brochures, information about schools, community relocation information, etc. Throw in a current real estate magazine that shows homes for sale in your area.

Candidate Confirmation of Interest Call

After the candidate has returned home, the chair or the recruiter should reconnect with them by phone to ascertain several things from the candidate. First, give them a sense of where you are in the hiring process and what the rest of the process will look like. As the committee wraps up its due diligence, the chair or recruiter needs to explore the following with each candidate:

- Level of Interest – At the start of this search, some candidates may have been actively looking for a job while others were merely "open to listening." What is this candidate's true level of interest in this opportunity? On a scale of 1-5, are they "really" interested or are they "just kicking the tires"?

- Primary Motivators – What would potentially motivate the candidate to leave their current work and join your congregation? Hopefully, it is more than money. Are they looking for a full-time pulpit? Are they looking for an opportunity to continue their education? Are they looking for strong leadership from their elders? What gets them excited?

- Potential Issues – Assuming that the job offer would be market-competitive, what would keep them from accepting your offer? Are they stuck in a long-term lease? Does their spouse need a job? Do they really love where they are? Can they envision themselves making the move?

You do not want to "lead the candidate on" or create the impression that they have the job. The committee just needs to know if the candidate would really be prepared to make a career change. This call will also help uncover issues that might need to be factored into a future job offer if things progress to that point.

Search Committee Visit (optional)

There are two primary reasons to consider a search committee visit to the finalists' current congregations at this time: 1) there was insufficient material available in the Round 3 review or 2) after the in-person interviews, the committee is struggling to differentiate the finalists.

A visit to each remaining candidate's congregation can provide valuable insights as the committee prepares to make its final decisions. However, in making a visit, the committee needs to take care that they don't create an issue for the candidate. Remember, there is no guarantee that you will eventually hire this person.

While some might want to make a "surprise" visit, I would highly discourage it. You never want to take the chance that your presence might somehow distract the candidate from the delivery of their message. Also, it would be a shame to travel to their congregation only to find that they have a guest speaker or "special" service that day. For these reasons and many others, discuss the visit with the candidate ahead of time and stress your sensitivity to the need for discretion.

Consider taking just a subset of the committee or splitting the visit over several weeks into smaller teams. When you go, don't sit together as a "search committee" or do anything that might draw attention to yourselves.

Avoid meeting with the candidate before the class or service. Again, you don't want to do anything that would distract from their delivery of the lesson that they have prepared. If you meet with them at all, do it after worship and away from the church building to minimize the chance of creating a problem for them.

Observe not only the content and delivery of the candidate's lesson, but also look for how they interact with the congregation. Are the members engaged in the sermon? Does the minister work the auditorium before and after worship to greet members and guests? How does the style of their delivery match what your congregation would expect or appreciate?

Candidate Rejections

If the committee has firmly eliminated a candidate (based on something in their interview or search committee visit), the recruiter or chair should send them a letter thanking them for their interest in the position, but letting them know that committee is moving forward in a different direction at this time.

| CHAPTER 11 |

Round 5 - Nomination

Once the in-person interviews and site visits are completed, the committee should meet again to review the Round 4 results.

 Prayer

As you prepare to select a nominee, spend time in prayer at the outset of the nomination meeting. Pray for wisdom, humility and brotherly love as you approach your final deliberations. Pray for the candidates by name and offer praise for something good about each one of them.

On a candidate-by-candidate basis, again review the notes made during the reference calls, lesson reviews and site visits. Discuss the committee's observations from the in-person interviews and any information gained from the chair's call to confirm the candidate's level of interest. Following those reports, the committee should assess their current status and see if they are ready to nominate a candidate.

The Committee should pause at this point to reconsider the charge the elders delivered at the initial committee meeting. Make sure that your next actions will be in accord with your charge. In most cases, I believe that it is best for the search committee to reach a <u>single consensus nominee</u>.

Single Candidate – The committee should forward a single name to the elders and congregation for their consideration. When a committee forwards multiple names for a congregational visit, it can indicate division or uncertainty on the part of the committee. Some members of the congregation will undoubtedly like one candidate more than another and may be upset that "their guy" was not selected. The elders and the congregation have entrusted the committee with the responsibility of finding the next minister and that is what the committee should do.

Consensus Nominee – The elders may have indicated in their charge that they wanted a unanimous decision on the part of the committee. If that is so, then the committee should deliberate until it can reach a unanimous decision. In most cases, however, I recommend that the committee reach a "consensus decision" where the vast majority of the committee agrees on a particular candidate.

The committee should heed the concerns of dissenting committee members (especially if they are doctrinal in nature) and work for unity, but also realize that people of good conscience might sometimes disagree. Dissenting committee members should either support the decision of the committee or consider resigning from the committee if the disagreement is too severe.

Ultimately, the committee is in the best position, with all of the information, to make the best decision on the proper nominee for the position.

Prayer

Having arrived at a nominee, spend time in prayer before the close of the nomination meeting. Pray for the nominee, their family and their current work or congregation. Pray that if it is God's will, that the Introduction Phase go smoothly and that the nominee will have a peace about accepting the eventual job offer. Likewise, pray that if this is not God's will that He will work providentially to keep the nominee from accepting.

Round 5 Candidate Rejections

Unlike prior rounds, the committee will not send out any further rejection letters until your nominee has accepted the final job offer. Should something fall through with the nominee, the committee will want the flexibility to return to a remaining finalist for further discussions and to restart the congregational visit process with one of them.

Section IV – The Introduction Phase

 "So Barnabas went to Tarsus to look for Saul and when he had found him, he brought him to Antioch. For a whole year they met with the church and taught a great many people. And in Antioch the disciples were first called Christians." – Acts 11:25-26

If the committee has indeed found a nominee, then it is time to introduce the nominee and the congregation to each other. That introduction should start with a report to the elders and then working with them to develop an offer letter. Once the elders are on board, the rest of this phase is spent helping the nominee and their family determine if the position, the congregation and the community are the right fit for them through a weekend-long congregational visit. This phase will conclude when the job offer is accepted.

CHAPTER 12

Engaging the Elders

Once the committee has a nominee, the chair should meet with the elders to provide them with a complete update on the committee's work and current status. The chair should provide them with the name and application packet for the nominee. It might also be helpful to provide the elders with copies of the notes made in the referencing phase and any other information that the committee might have gathered about the nominee.

If there are any serious reservations still lingering within the committee regarding the nominee, they should be brought to the elders' attention at this time as well. The chair and the elders need to acknowledge any concerns and make sure that there is still agreement on moving forward.

Ask the elders to be actively involved in the congregational visit and provide them with a proposed itinerary for the weekend. Let them know that the itinerary will be finalized once the nominee has been contacted and has had an opportunity to provide input on the details.

Beyond planning for the congregational visit, the next most important task for the elders and search committee is the creation of a market-competitive (and hopefully irresistible) job offer in the form of an offer letter.

Offer Letter

Working under the assumption that the elders will approve of the nominee after they meet with them during the congregational visit, the elders and chair should begin work on the job offer and related offer letter ahead of the actual visit itself. The elders and chair should be prepared to extend the job offer at the end of the congregational visit.

In preparing the offer, the chair should refer back to their notes from the confirmation of interest call and pay particular attention to the nominee's primary motivators and potential issues. If at all possible, the congregation should include support for their primary motivators (e.g., a tuition reimbursement plan if they are driven by the desire to continue their education). To the extent you can, address their potential issues (e.g., if they are trapped in a long-term lease, help them cover the cost of cancellation). At a minimum, the job offer should include:

- A market-competitive salary
  - See the salary range guidance suggestions in Chapter 1 for help with an offer amount.
- A market-competitive benefits package
  - Vacation time
  - Holiday time
  - Sick leave
  - Health insurance
  - Retirement contribution or matching
- An overview of the supporting resources that will be provided
  - Secretarial support
  - Technology resources (laptop, home office, etc.)
  - Vehicle or mileage reimbursement policy
  - Allowance for books, training and study materials
  - Continuing education opportunities

- A transition plan to help cover the costs of relocating
  - Moving expense allowance
  - Temporary housing allowance

Sometimes there are timing differences between how one congregation pays versus another. Consider the inclusion of a "signing bonus" to help them cover any payroll transition periods.

The purpose of the offer letter is to clearly reduce the specifics of the job offer to written form so that there can be no doubt about what is or is not included in the employment offer. The letter should also incorporate by reference a final copy of the job description to be fulfilled by the nominee.

Generally speaking, the offer letter is not intended to be treated as a contract, but if you include certain phrases or fail to include others, the courts might treat it as one. Be careful to avoid any statements that might be construed as establishing a term of employment (e.g., "We expect you to be here for many years to come...") You also need to include a specific reference that their employment is an "at will" relationship that either party can end at any time for any reason.

Be sure the letter also includes a reasonable timeframe for them to respond. If you know that they are considering multiple offers, don't give them a tight deadline that backs them into a corner on the other offers. At the same time, don't make the deadline so long that it would create a problem if you had to return to your other Round 4 finalists for some reason. A ten- to fourteen-day timeframe is typically sufficient.

Once the offer letter has been drafted, make sure that the elders review and approve of the final package before it is given to the nominee at the conclusion of their congregational visit.

| CHAPTER 13 |

Congregational Visit

Once the elders have approved of the nominee, the committee should start organizing a weekend visit full of fellowship activities, tours and meetings focused on the various needs and interests of the nominee's family. This will require careful planning to ensure that the nominee receives all of the information that they will need to make an informed decision.

Preparation

Nominee Invitation

The chair should connect with the nominee and let them know that they are the committee's pick for the position and that the elders have approved of the nomination. The chair should then coordinate a weekend that will work for the nominee and their family to visit. Set the date two, three, or even four weeks out to allow all parties adequate time to prepare.

As part of the invitation, provide the nominee with a proposed itinerary for their weekend. Let them know that the weekend will be focused on helping them meet the congregation and helping their family determine if this is the right fit for them. Invite their feedback on the itinerary and be prepared to make adjustments that might better suit their needs and interests.

Be sure to clearly note any speaking, teaching or preaching responsibilities that the nominee might have during the

weekend. If they will be preaching, provide them with a sample order of worship and ask them for input on things like scripture reading and song selection to coincide with their lesson.

As with the Round 3 trip, the committee should coordinate the nominee's travel details and pay for the trip and any incidental costs. As a general rule, do not try to house the nominee with a member of the congregation. Get them a nice hotel room. Their family will need time during the weekend to be alone and discuss what they have experienced. Also, if they are flying in from another city, be sure to provide them with access to a car as well so that they can get out and explore the community if time permits.

It might also be helpful to ask one of your women leaders in the congregation (e.g., an elder's wife or minister's wife) to reach out to the spouse of your nominee. Let the spouse know that as a fellow wife of a church leader she is praying for them. She can share with the nominee's wife why she loves living in your community or worshipping with your congregation. It can go a long way towards helping the spouse feel like they have a connection in the congregation.

Nominee Announcement

About two weeks before the scheduled visit, the chair or the elders should provide an update to the congregation. Reiterate the basics of the elder's charge to the committee. Talk about the process that the committee has gone through to get to this point. Tell the congregation that the committee has selected a nominee to be the next minister, but that it is important for the nominee and congregation to meet each other before a final offer is extended.

Announce the nominee's name. Give a brief biography on them and tell why the committee believes they are the right person. It might be helpful to again repeat some of the comments gathered in the referencing process.

Talk about the upcoming congregational visit. Outline the agenda for the weekend and highlight opportunities for the members to meet the nominee. Encourage their full participation and ask them to get behind the nominee and really make them feel welcome.

Prayer

Ask the congregation to pray for the nominee and their family as they weigh this important decision.

Also, ask the congregation to refrain from posting anything on social media until after the nominee has been officially hired. If something was to fall through and the nominee was not hired for some reason, you would not want to unnecessarily upset the nominee's current congregation.

Planning

The committee as a whole should take the lead on planning and hosting the various meetings and events of the visit weekend.

Try to create a blend between meetings within the congregation and time spent in the community. Help them see why they might want to live and worship in your community.

If there are meetings on the schedule that would take the nominee away from their family, consider having counter-balancing activities for the rest of the family.

Be mindful of the family's needs and interests. If you don't know what these might be, ask the nominee. Consider things such as:

- Does the nominee or their family have any particular hobbies (e.g., hiking, tennis, golf, etc.)? Give them a quick tour of your local resources.
- Will the nominee's spouse be looking for a job? Help them connect with potential employers while in town.

- Do they have children who play sports or are involved in the arts? Be sure to set up a tour of the appropriate athletic facilities, band rooms or theaters. Help them meet some of the local coaches and organizers of those events.
- Do their children attend public or private schools? Give them a tour of your local schools if at all possible.

It is important that the nominee gets to meet broad cross-sections of the congregation. It is also important that they and their family get to meet with people their own age.

- Consider hosting some sort of church-wide reception or meal that would allow everyone a chance to meet with the nominee.
- To help the family get a feel for whom some of their friends might be, consider hosting an age-specific social event. For instance, if they have young children, get a group of families from that age group together for a family game night. Or, if they have a teen in the youth group, consider getting the teens to host an event for them.

Nominee Visit Itinerary

Friday
- Nominee arrival at their hotel (5:00)
  - Gift basket waiting in the room with items for each member of the family.
- Dinner with the search committee, elders, ministry team and all of their respective families (6:30)

Saturday
- Breakfast with nominee and the chair (8:00)
  - Talk about the weekend's events.
- Meeting with elders (9:00)

- Chance for the elders and nominee to ask questions of each other .
- Family facility tour (10:30)
  - Family joins nominee at the church for a quick tour
- Community tour (11:00)
  - Focus on schools, parks, hobbies, points of interest, shopping, industry, etc.
  - Allow time for stops at places that would be of particular interest.
- Lunch on-the-go between tours - OR - Lunch with a non-peer age group (12:00)
  - If it is lunch on-the-go, find a place unique to the culture and feel of the community.
  - If it is lunch with a non-peer age group, match the nominee up with whatever age group is not their peer age group (i.e., older members for younger candidates).
- Real estate tour (1:30)
  - Connect them with a real estate agent ahead of time so they can show them homes or apartments of interest to them.
- Free time (3:30)
  - This is their time to relax or get out and drive around the community on their own.
- Dinner/social evening with their peer age group (6:00)
- Evening wrap-up (9:00)
  - Bring the evening to a close at a reasonable time so that the nominee will be well rested for their Sunday responsibilities.

Sunday

- Bible class & worship
  - Consider having a combined Bible class for the appropriate age groups and asking the nominee to teach that class (i.e., youth ministers would teach the youth

group, pulpit ministers would teach a combined adult class, etc.).

- If they are preaching or leading worship, the chair or an elder should introduce the nominee and their family to the congregation.

- Church reception/pot-luck lunch after worship
- Wrap-up meeting with the search committee
  - Invite the nominee and their spouse in for a brief review meeting.
  - Give them a final chance to ask any questions that they might have.
- Extend the job offer
  - If an offer is not yet possible for some reason, reassure them of your continued interest and give them a timeframe of when they might hear from the congregation next.

CHAPTER 14

The Offer

Prior to the congregational visit, the chair and elders should have a conversation about who will deliver the actual offer and when that will take place.

Extending the Offer

Traditionally, many congregations have waited until after the congregational visit is over and then they send a copy of the offer in the following days. The person delivering the offer may or may not get the chance to walk the nominee through the offer before the nominee has had a chance to read it for themselves. Regardless, when delivered remotely, you will lose a lot of the personal dynamics that can really help you sell the offer.

I recommend that the chair or elders deliver the job offer at the conclusion of the congregational visit. Let them see your excitement and desire for them to accept. Walk them through the details of the compensation, benefits, etc. Focus on the areas that are of greatest importance to the nominee. Make sure you are on the same page before they leave to return home.

Don't expect a candidate to accept your offer on the spot. Most will want to take some time to pray about the offer and discuss it with their family and friends. Simply ask that they let you know something either way by the deadline outlined in the offer letter.

Offer Negotiation

Decide ahead of time how you will handle a counter offer from the nominee. Will you negotiate, or is your offer final?

Don't be offended if the nominee makes a counter offer. To some degree they are saying, "I really do want to come to your congregation but I need help making it all work."

In most cases, they are simply trying to do what is best for their family, their career and the church at large. Remember to "love your neighbor as yourself." What would you do if you were in their shoes?

Offer Rejection

If for some reason the candidate rejects the offer outright, then it is time to move forward with the remaining Round 4 finalists. Do not try to talk the candidate into accepting the position. They have weighed all of the factors and decided that this is not the right opportunity for them. Trying to convince them otherwise is both disrespectful of the candidate and potentially damaging to the congregation. The last thing you want is a minister or family who had to be talked into coming to your congregation.

If the opportunity presents itself, it might be helpful to do a quick debrief with the candidate when they turn you down. Was there something in the process, the offer or the congregation that gave them pause and caused them to say no? There might be something you need to address before you bring in the next candidate.

Offer Acceptance

When the nominee calls to accept the offer (and the initial celebration is over), work out a starting date that is fair to them, their current congregation and your congregation. It is not unusual for ministry start dates to be 2-3 months after offer acceptance.

Once you have an accepted offer with the nominee, the remaining candidates should receive a copy of the Round 4 rejection letter from the recruiter or chair thanking them for their interest in the position, but letting them know that the committee is moving forward in a different direction at this time.

Candidate Information Disposal

After the offer is accepted, you need to help the committee members dispose of any hard copies of documents that they may still have. Anything that would contain personal information about your candidates, a list of candidates, etc. should be gathered together and destroyed by the committee secretary through shredding or incineration.

Section V – The On-Boarding Phase

"Let each of you look not only to his own interests, but also to the interests of others." – Philippians 2:4 ESV

Prayer

Pray for the new minister and their family as they prepare for this time of transition. Pray for their ministry to be effective with your congregation. Pray for the congregation that they are leaving.

Most search committees stop once they nominate a candidate or get an acceptance to the job offer. They figure that their work is done and it is now time for the elders, the church staff or someone else to take over. I would encourage a different approach.

The search committee should stay engaged as a team with the new minister until they are firmly established within the congregation and community. The committee should:

- ☐ Help them with their relocation,
- ☐ Help them meet people and establish relationships, and
- ☐ Help them develop a plan for their first few months (which so often sets the tone for their entire career with the congregation).

CHAPTER 15

Relocation Support Plan

Moving is a stressful time for any family. Your new minister has to wrap up life in one location while laying the foundation for a life in your community. Appoint someone from the search committee to become a relocation resource for your new minister. Do everything you can to support and assist them with this transition. Make them feel welcomed and loved. Here are just a few ideas where you can help:

- **Temporary Housing** – Find the minister a spare bedroom if they need a temporary place to stay while going back and forth to work out details for their move.
- **Home** – Help them connect with a real estate agent to find a new home.
- **Banks** – Take them to your local bank and introduce them to your banker.
- **Schools** – If they have school-age children, help them find a school and get registered.
- **Jobs** – If their spouse or kids need help finding a job, ask people in the congregation to be on the lookout for opportunities.
- **Sports teams or clubs** – If they have kids involved in scouts, sports or other activities, help them connect with troops, leagues and coaches.

When it comes time for the actual move, the search committee should get a team of church members to come and help unload the van, unpack boxes or haul away trash. Ask members to sign up for a meal and take turns providing dinner for the first week in their new home. Get someone to mow the yard or trim the shrubs. Do anything you can to help them feel welcomed and settled.

Personal Connections

You also need to help your minister establish relationships within the congregation and community at large. Appoint one or two members of the search committee to head up this task. Have one member focus on congregational connections and the other focus on community connections. Here are a few ideas for both areas:

- **Congregational**
    - Picture Directory — Provide them with a church directory before they start so they can start memorizing faces and names.
    - Familial Relationships — If your congregation has a lot of related members, provide them with a list of these relationships to help them learn the congregation even faster.
    - Peer Group — Organize recurring social activities for the new minister's age group.
    - Demographic Groups — Invite the minister to activities being held for all age groups (e.g., young-at-heart, boomers, merry middles, millennials, young professionals, etc.).

- **Community**
    - Civic Groups — If any members of the congregation are also members of a civic group (e.g., the Chamber of Commerce, Rotary, Kiwanis, Lions, etc.), ask them to take the new minister to a meeting as their guest.
    - Other Ministers — If you have other Church of Christ congregations in town, ask one of your ministers or

elders to take the new minister around and introduce them.

- Hospitals and nursing homes – If the new minister will have visitation responsibilities, take them to the facilities and introduce them to the staff.

CHAPTER 16

Startup

The First Day

The first day of any job can be both exciting and stressful. Eliminate some of that stress by anticipating the most common questions and then doing all you can as a committee to make that first day flow smoothly. For instance:

- Clean their office before they arrive.
- Set up their technology and have it ready to go (e.g., PC setup, e-mail account, phone extension, cell phone, etc.).
- Have an IT person stop by and see if they need any help.
- Have all of their HR paperwork ready (W2, payroll direct deposit, health insurance, employee handbook, policy manual, etc.).
- Give them a set of keys to the building and show them how to work the alarm.
- Have an elder, a minister or the search committee chair take them to lunch.
- Have their business cards waiting for them.
- Have someone help them carry and unpack their boxes and books.
- Allow them time to settle into their office.
- Reintroduce them to the church staff and give them time to visit.
- Clarify the rest of the schedule for the first week.

The First 100 Days

It is a little cliché and there are lots of books and articles about "the first hundred days," but the first few weeks and months of any new job truly are very important. In many cases, the minister will set the tone for their entire career with the congregation. The elders and/or search committee should work with the new minister to come up with a plan to accomplish the following within those first hundred days:

- People
  - Develop a plan to interact with all of the various Bible classes, small groups or age groups (young-at-heart, merry middles, young marrieds, etc.).
  - Meet the deacons and learn what they do within their area of ministry.
  - Establish a visitation plan to meet the chronically ill and shut-ins.
- Teaching
  - Teach or preach excellent lessons the first few months. Encourage them to reuse lessons that were successful at their last congregation and improve upon them.
- History
  - Read any books or historical documents that might exist about the congregation.
  - Read the minutes from the last couple of years of elders' meetings.
- Administration
  - Establish strong working relationships with the elders.
  - Review the church budget and understand the congregation's programs.
  - Learn the recurring schedules (bulletin deadlines, worship planning, etc.).

Avoid any urge to implement grand new ideas or sweeping changes during these first hundred days. This is about helping the minister settle into the congregation, not the reverse.

Conclusion

In hindsight, it would have been wonderful if Luke had included a chapter in Acts about how to find a new minister. Or why couldn't Paul have also written to Timothy or Titus to tell them how to appoint a replacement minister? Unfortunately, (or perhaps in God's wisdom) we don't have anything like that.

Through the autonomy of the local congregations, we have all had to figure out the hiring process for ourselves. Some groups have done a better job at this than others. It is my hope that congregations will find at least some portion of this handbook helpful in their search process.

My prayer for each congregation and minister would be that they have long-term, productive relationships together. That collectively we would fulfill the mission of Christ to seek and save the lost. And that one day we will all be united in our home in heaven. May God bless you in your efforts.

Appendix A

Table of documents and templates available at MinisterMatch.com

Appendix B

Minister Match offers a number of webinars and workshops to train your congregation on the Minister Hiring Process. For additional information on these and other training opportunities, please go to http://www.ministermatch.com/training.

The Role of the Elders in the Search Process

A successful minister search begins with clear, effective leadership from the elders of the congregation. In this 60-minute webinar we explore the minister search process from an elder's point of view. Specifically, we cover:

- The importance of making the right hire
- An overview of the Minister Hiring Process
- The role of the elders in a search
- Defining the position
- Forming a search committee
- Supporting and equipping the search committee
- Creating a "charge" for the committee
- Working with your committee
- Receiving the nominee
- Crafting the job offer.

Attend this webinar BEFORE you start your search!

The Role of the Search Committee Member

The simple fact is that most congregations fail to provide their search committees with any real training about how to do their job. In this 60-minute webinar we provide search committee members with a realistic overview of the task before them and provide practical instruction about how to proceed through the process. This introductory webinar will cover:

- The importance of making the right hire
- An overview of the Minister Hiring Process
- The role of a search committee member
- The importance of confidentiality
- Planning the search
- Developing a candidate recruiting strategy
- An overview of the selection process
- Fulfilling your "charge" from the elders.

Attend this webinar as you start your search!

The Search Process Workshop

This on-site, half-day workshop presents a step-by-step guide to the Minister Hiring Process™ and helps the committee lay the foundation for a successful search. The workshop can be tailored to the appropriate audience as well as to the target for the search process (e.g., pulpit vs. non-pulpit ministers).

In addition to the topics discussed in the Search Committee webinar, we typically cover advanced topics such as:

- Wrapping up the planning process
- The job description
- Writing effective ads and where to place them
- The congregational survey
- The candidate questionnaire

- Handling internal candidates
- Developing a recruiting plan
- Identifying networking sources
- Building a prospect list
- Practicing the "cold call"
- Writing better interview questions
- Details of the selection process.

Bonus #1 – 10 Free copies of *The Search Committee Handbook – The Step-by-Step Guide to Hiring Your Next Minister.* — A $250 value.

Bonus #2 – As part of this workshop, the committee receives unlimited access to the tools and templates section of the MinisterMatch.com website. This toolkit is full of the checklists, letters, agendas, sample forms, and sample questions that will help ease the workload on the committee and ensure the success of your search. — A $450 value.

Made in the USA
Middletown, DE
20 September 2023

38866424R00066